Impressum
Verlag: BABADADA GmbH, Nedderfeld 112 , 22529 Hamburg
Geschäftsführer / Verlagsleitung: Harald Hof
Druck: Books on Demand GmbH, In de Tarpen 42, 22848 Norderstedt

Imprint
Publisher: BABADADA GmbH, Nedderfeld 112 , 22529 Hamburg, Germany
Managing Director / Publishing direction: Harald Hof
Print: Books on Demand GmbH, In de Tarpen 42, 22848 Norderstedt

school
école

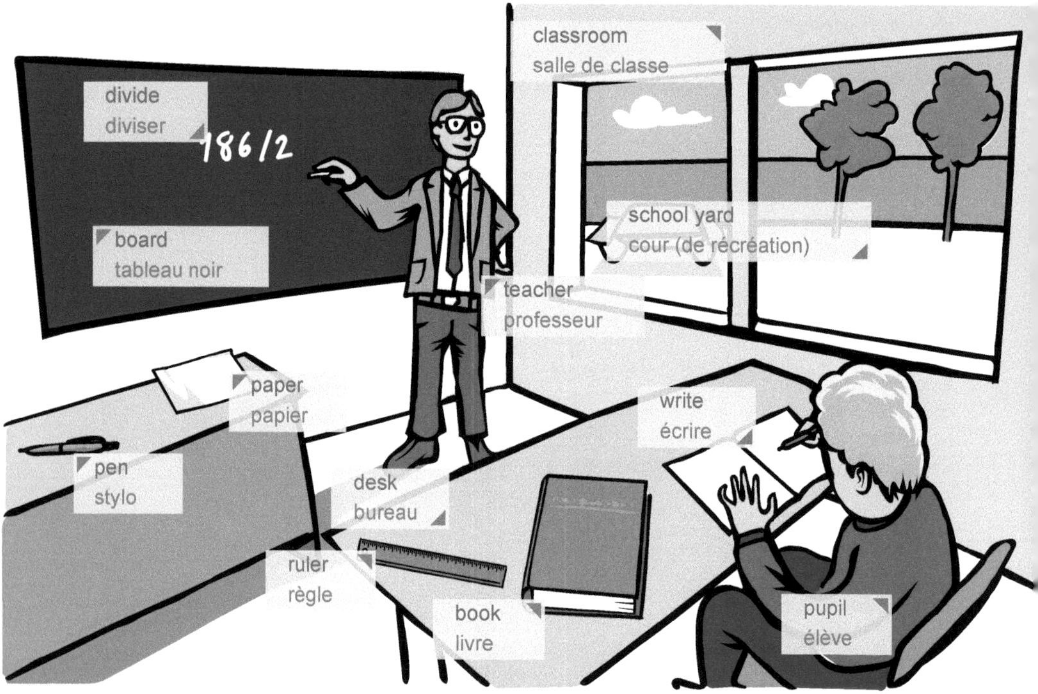
classroom
salle de classe
divide
diviser
186/2
board
tableau noir
school yard
cour (de récréation)
teacher
professeur
paper
papier
write
écrire
pen
stylo
desk
bureau
ruler
règle
book
livre
pupil
élève

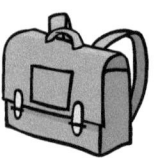

satchel
cartable

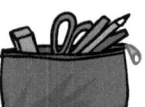

pencil case
trousse

pencil
crayon

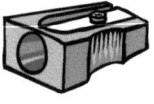

pencil sharpener
taille-crayon

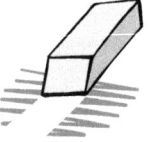

rubber
gomme

drawing pad
carnet à dessin

drawing

dessin

paintbrush

pinceau

paint box

boîte de peinture

scissors

ciseaux

glue

colle

exercise book

cahier d'exercices

homework

devoirs

number

chiffre

add

additionner

subtract

soustraire

multiply

multiplier

calculate

calculer

letter

lettre

alphabet

alphabet

word

mot

text

texte

read

lire

chalk

craie

lesson

leçon

register

livre de classe

examination

examen

certificate

certificat

school uniform

uniforme scolaire

education

formation

encyclopedia

lexique

university

université

microscope

microscope

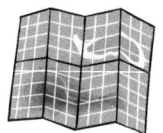

map

carte

waste-paper basket

corbeille à papier

school - école

travel
voyage

hotel
hôtel
Grand
hostel
auberge
ROOMS
currency exchange office
bureau de change
CHANGE
suitcase
valise
car
voiture

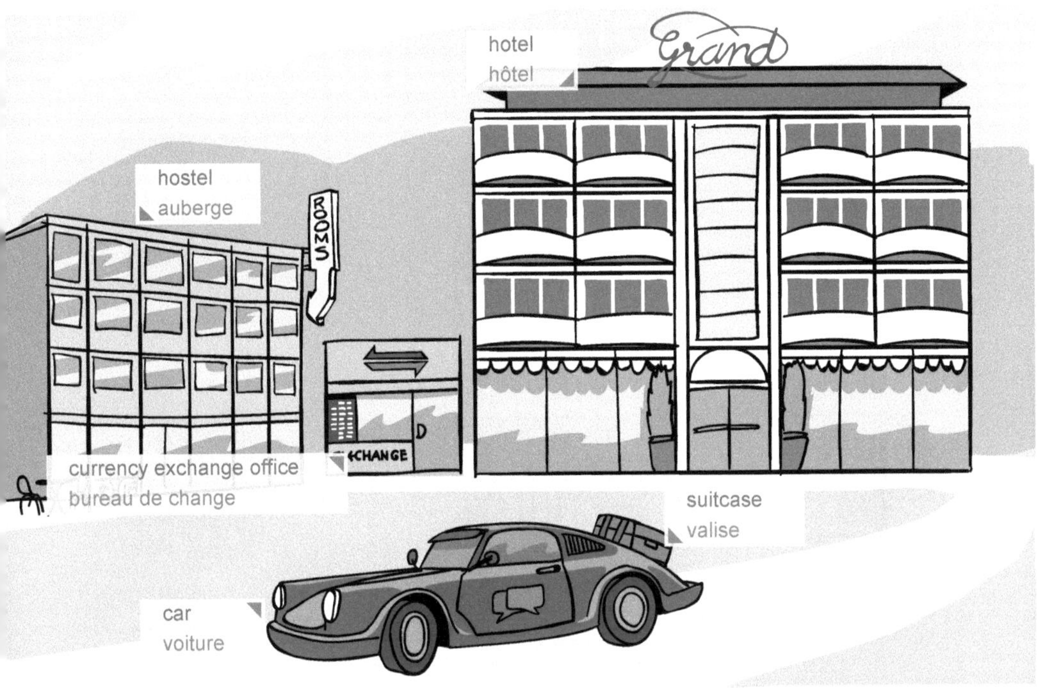

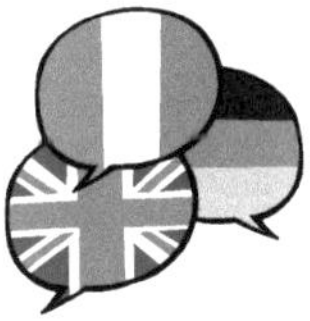

language
langue

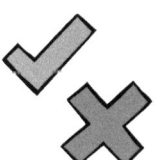

yes / no
oui / non

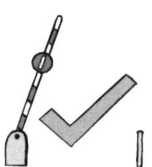

Okay
d'accord

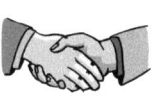

hello
Salut

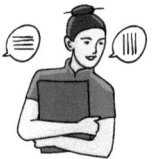

translator
interprète

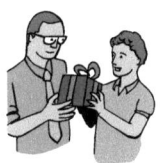

Thank you
merci

how much is…?

Combien coûte…?

I don´t get it

Je ne comprends pas

problem

problème

Good evening!

Bonsoir !

Good morning!

Bonjour !

Good night!

Bonne nuit !

goodbye

Au revoir

direction

direction

luggage

bagages

bag

sac

backpack

sac-à-dos

guest

hôte

room

pièce

sleeping bag

sac de couchage

tent

tente

tourist information

office de tourisme

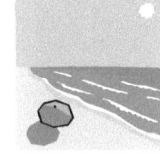

beach

plage

credit card

carte de crédit

breakfast

petit-déjeuner

lunch

déjeuner

dinner

dîner

Ticket

billet

elevator

ascenseur

stamp

timbre

border

frontière

customs

douane

embassy

ambassade

visa

visa

passport

passeport

transport

transport

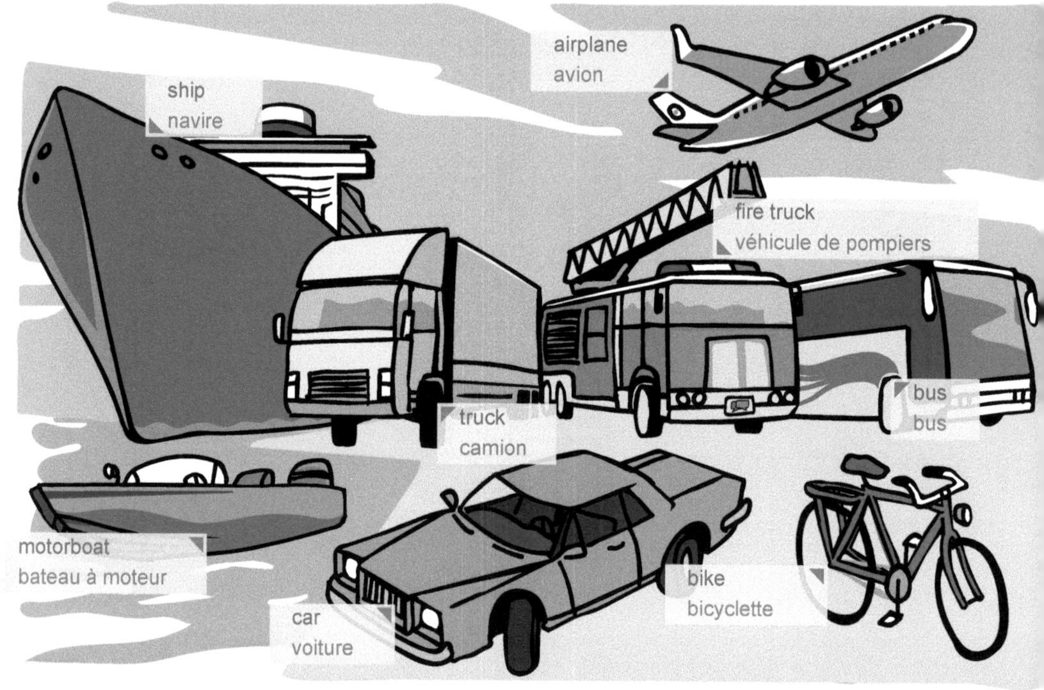

airplane
avion
ship
navire
fire truck
véhicule de pompiers
truck
camion
bus
bus
motorboat
bateau à moteur
bike
bicyclette
car
voiture

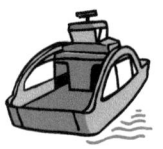

ferry

ferry

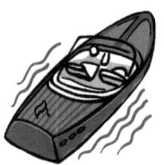

boat

barque

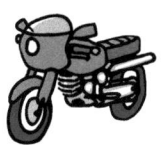

motorbike

moto

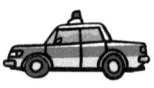

police car

voiture de police

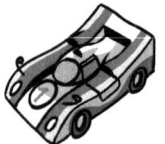

racing car

voiture de course

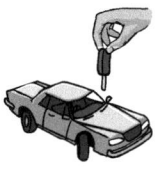

rental car

voiture de location

car sharing

auto-partage

tow truck

voiture de remorquage

garbage truck

benne à ordures

engine

moteur

fuel

essence

fuel station

station d'essence

traffic sign

panneau indicateur

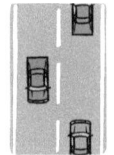

traffic

trafic

traffic jam

embouteillage

parking lot

parking

train station

gare

tracks

rails

train

train

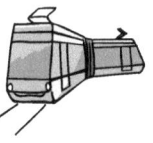

tram

tramway

wagon

wagon

helicopter
hélicoptère

airport
aéroport

tower
tour

passenger
passager

container
conteneur

carton
carton

cart
chariot

basket
corbeille

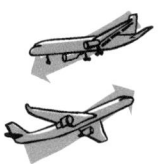

take off / land
décoller / atterrir

city

ville

village
village

city center
centre-ville

house
maison

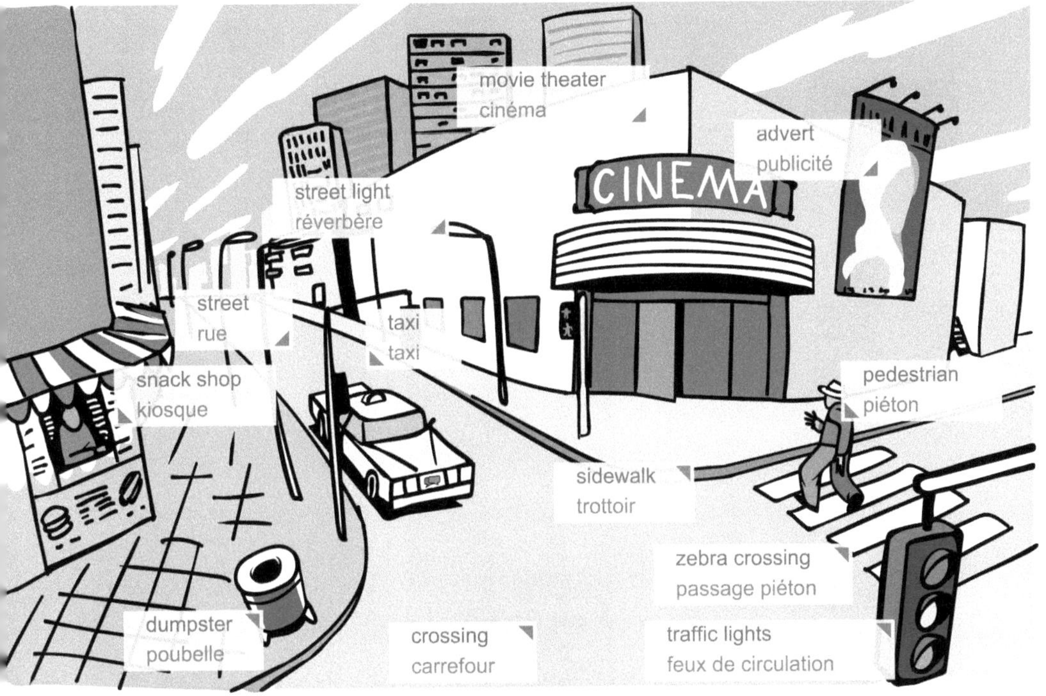

movie theater
cinéma

advert
publicité

street light
réverbère

CINEMA

street
rue

taxi
taxi

snack shop
kiosque

pedestrian
piéton

sidewalk
trottoir

zebra crossing
passage piéton

dumpster
poubelle

crossing
carrefour

traffic lights
feux de circulation

hut

cabane

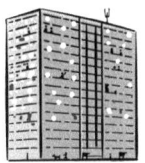

apartment

appartement

train station

gare

city hall

mairie

museum

musée

school

école

university

université

bank

banque

hospital

hôpital

hotel

hôtel

pharmacy

pharmacie

office

bureau

book shop

librairie

shop

magasin

flower shop

fleuriste

supermarket

supermarché

market

marché

department store

grand magasin

fishmonger's shop

poissonnerie

mall

centre commercial

harbor

port

park

parc

bench

banque

bridge

pont

stairs

escaliers

subway

métro

tunnel

tunnel

bus stop

arrêt de bus

bar

bar

restaurant

restaurant

postbox

boîte à lettres

street sign

panneau indicateur

parking meter

parcmètre

zoo

zoo

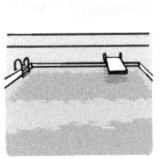

swimming pool

piscine

mosque

mosquée

farm

ferme

pollution

pollution

cemetery

cimetière

church

église

playground

aire de jeux

temple

temple

landscape

paysage

leaf
feuille

signpost
panneau indicateur

path
chemin

meadow
pré

stone
pierre

hiker
randonneur

tree
arbre

river
rivière

grass
herbe

flower
fleur

valley

vallée

hill

montagne

lake

lac

forest

forêt

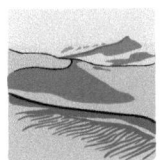

desert

désert

volcano

volcan

castle

château

rainbow

arc-en-ciel

mushroom

champignon

palm tree

palmier

mosquito

moustique

fly

mouche

ant

fourmis

bee

abeille

spider

araignée

landscape - paysage

beetle

coléoptère

frog

grenouille

squirrel

écureuil

hedgehog

hérisson

hare

lièvre

owl

chouette

bird

oiseau

swan

cygne

boar

sanglier

deer

cerf

moose

élan

dam

barrage

wind turbine

éolienne

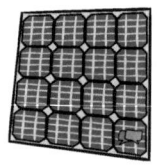

solar panel

panneau solaire

climate

climat

landscape - paysage

restaurant
restaurant

waiter
serveur
menu
menu
chair
chaise
soup
soupe
pizza
pizza
cutlery
couverts
tablecloth
nappe

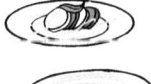

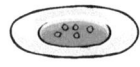

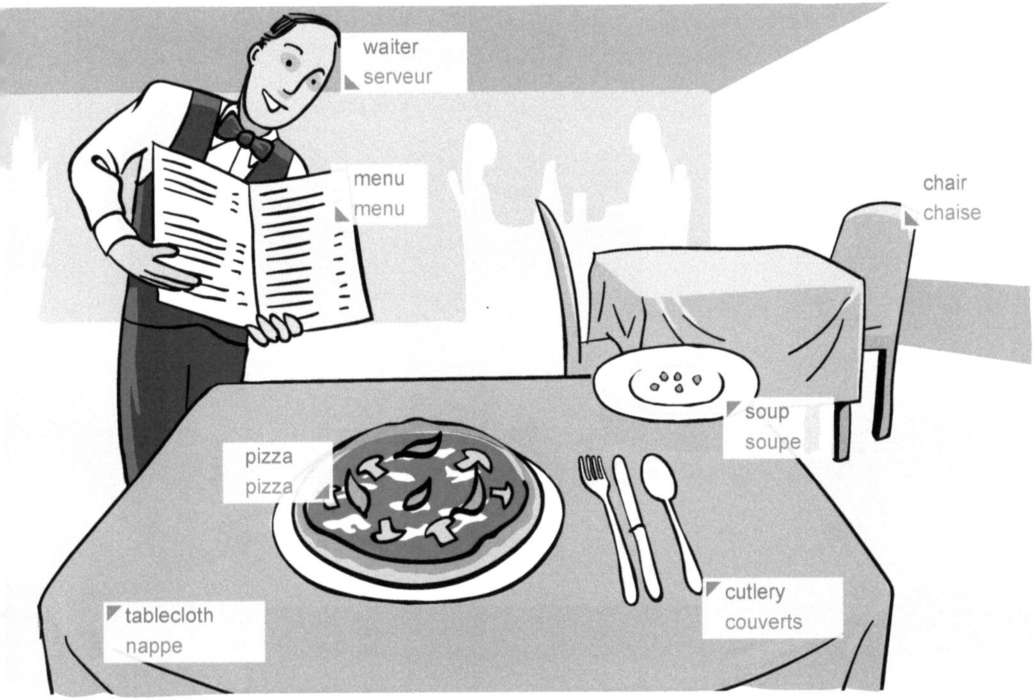

starter
hors d'œuvre

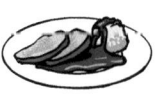

main course
plat principal

dessert
dessert

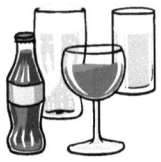

drinks
boissons

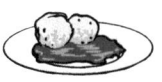

food
alimentation

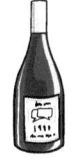

bottle
bouteille

fast food

fast-food

street food

plats à emporter

teapot

théière

sugar bowl

sucrier

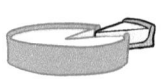

portion

portion

espresso machine

machine à expresso

high chair

chaise haute

bill

facture

tray

plateau

knife

couteau

fork

fourchette

spoon

cuillère

teaspoon

cuillère à thé

serviette

serviette

glass

verre

restaurant - restaurant

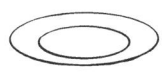

plate

assiette

soup plate

assiette à soupe

saucer

soucoupe

sauce

sauce

salt shaker

salière

pepper mill

moulin à poivre

vinegar

vinaigre

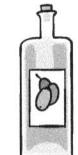

oil

huile

spices

épices

ketchup

ketchup

mustard

moutarde

mayonnaise

mayonnaise

supermarket
supermarché

special offer
offre promotionnelle
FOR
customer
client
dairy products
produits laitiers
fruit
fruits
shopping cart
chariot

BUTCHERS

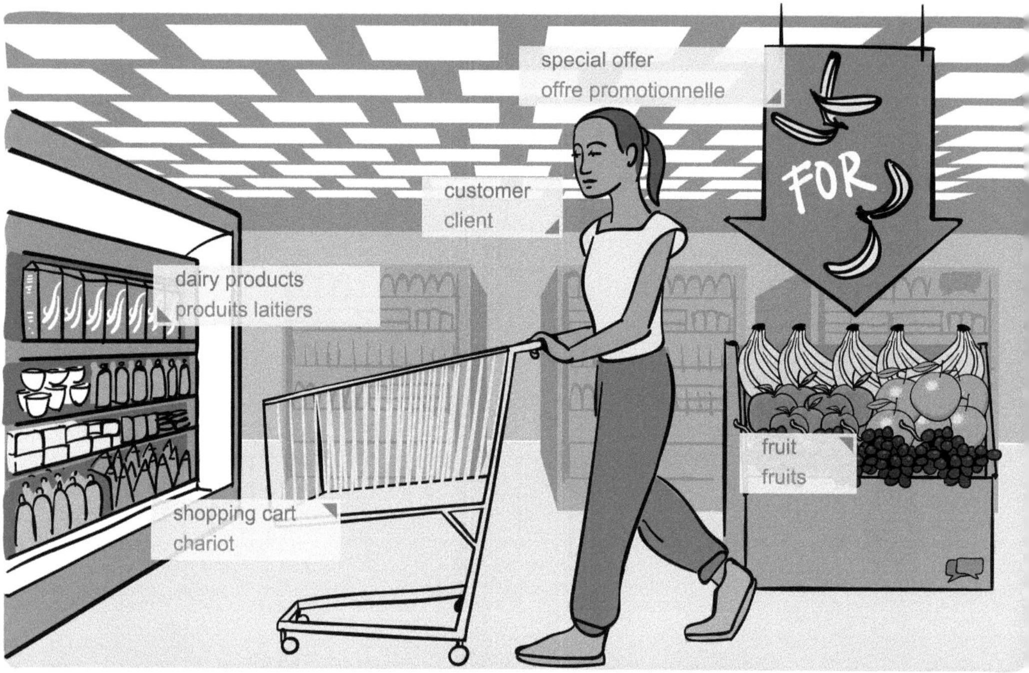

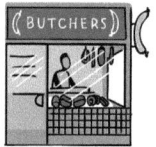

butcher's shop

boucherie

BAKERY

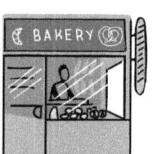

bakery

boulangerie

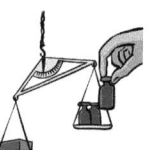

weigh

peser

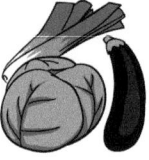

vegetables

légumes

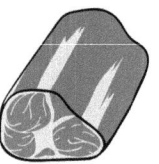

meat

viande

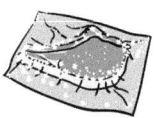

frozen food

aliments surgelés

cold cuts

charcuterie

canned food

conserves

detergent

poudre à lessive

candy

bonbons

household products

articles ménagers

cleaning products

détergents

sales representative

vendeuse

cash register

caisse

cashier

caissier

shopping list

liste d'achats

opening hours

heures d'ouverture

wallet

portefeuille

credit card

carte de crédit

bag

sac

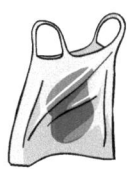

plastic bag

sac en plastique

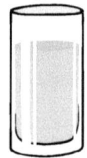

water

eau

juice

jus de fruit

milk

lait

coke

coca

wine

vin

beer

bière

alcohol

alcool

cocoa

chocolat chaud

tea

thé

coffee

café

espresso

expresso

cappuccino

cappuccino

banana

banane

apple

pomme

orange

orange

melon

melon

lemon

citron

carrot

carotte

garlic

ail

bamboo

bambou

onion

oignon

mushroom

champignon

nuts

noisettes

noodles

pâtes

spaghetti

spaghetti

rice

riz

salad

salade

fries

pommes frites

fried potatoes

pommes de terre rôties

pizza

pizza

hamburger

hamburger

sandwich

sandwich

escalope

escalope

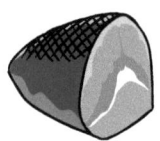

ham

jambon

salami

salami

sausage

saucisse

chicken

poulet

roast

rôti

fish

poisson

porridge oats

flocons d'avoine

muesli

muesli

cornflakes

cornflakes

flour

farine

croissant

croissant

bread roll

petits-pains

bread

pain

toast

pain grillé

cookies

biscuits

butter

beurre

curd

le fromage blanc

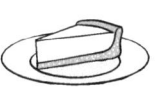

cake

gâteau

egg

œuf

fried egg

œuf au plat

cheese

fromage

ice cream

glace

sugar

sucre

honey

miel

jelly

confiture

nougat cream

crème nougat

curry

curry

farm
ferme

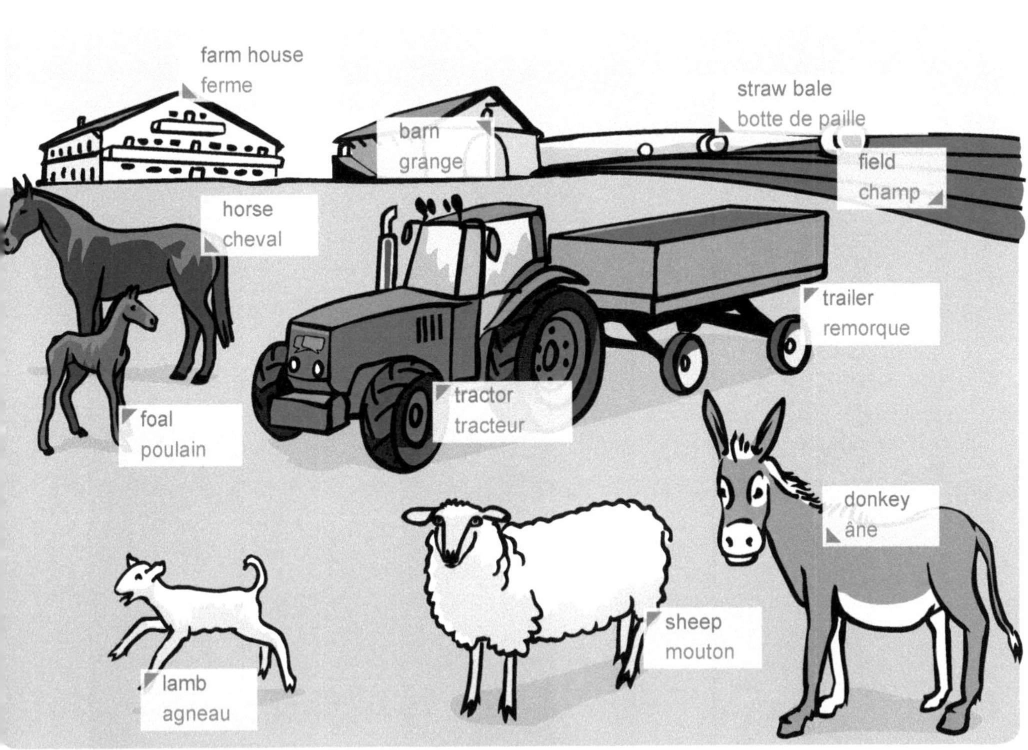
farm house
ferme
straw bale
botte de paille
barn
grange
field
champ
horse
cheval
trailer
remorque
tractor
tracteur
foal
poulain
donkey
âne
sheep
mouton
lamb
agneau

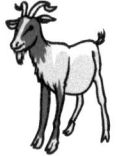

goat

chèvre

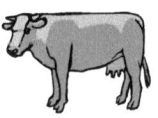

cow

vache

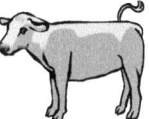

calf

veau

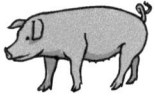

pig

porc

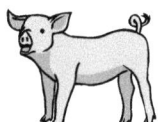

piglet

porcelet

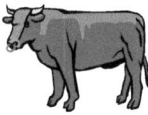

bull

taureau

goose

oie

duck

canard

chick

poussin

hen

poule

cockerel

coq

rat

rat

cat

chat

mouse

souris

ox

bœuf

dog

chien

dog house

chenil

garden hose

tuyau de jardin

watering can

arrosoir

scythe

faucheuse

plow

charrue

sickle

faucille

hoe

pioche

pitchfork

fourche

axe

hache

pushcart

brouette

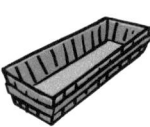

trough

cuve

milk can

pot à lait

sack

sac

fence

clôture

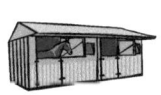

stable

étable

greenhouse

serre

soil

sol

seed

semences

fertilizer

engrais

combine harvester

moissonneuse-batteuse

harvest

récolter

harvest

récolte

yams

igname

wheat

blé

soya

soja

potato

pomme de terre

corn

maïs

rapeseed

colza

fruit tree

arbre fruitier

manioc

manioc

grain

céréales

house
maison

chimney
cheminée
roof
toit
downspout
gouttière
window
fenêtre
doorbell
sonnette
garage
garage
door
porte
trash can
poubelle
mailbox
boîte aux lettres
garden
jardin

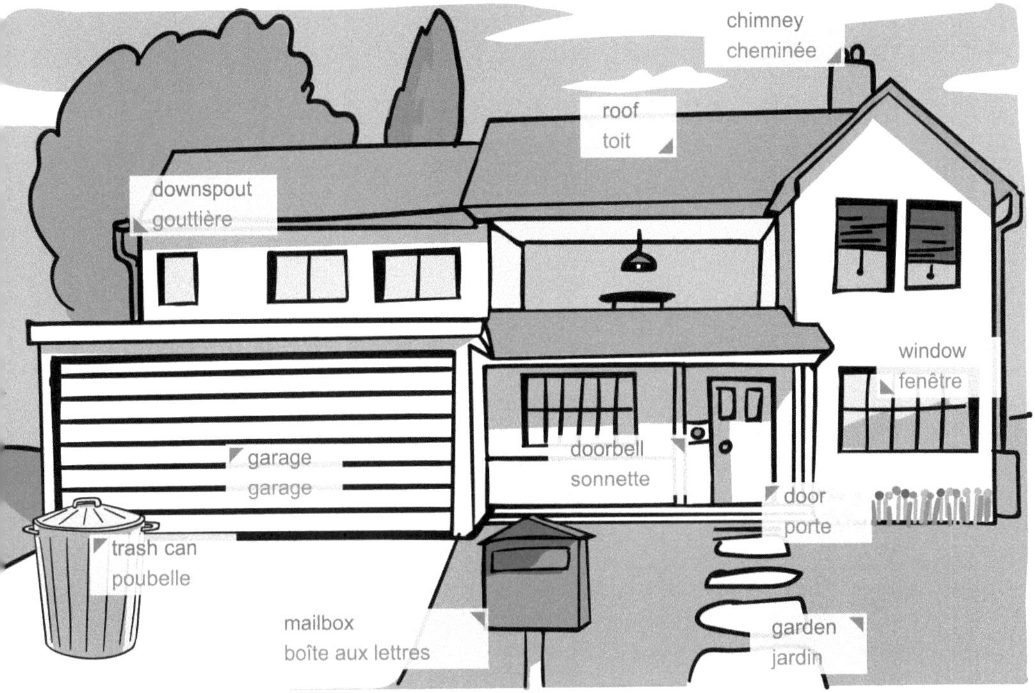

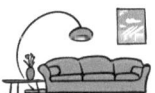

living room

salon

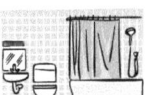

bathroom

salle de bain

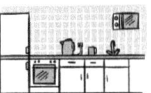

kitchen

cuisine

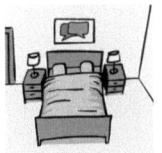

bedroom

chambre à coucher

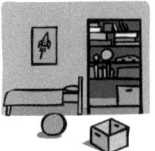

kids room

chambre d'enfant

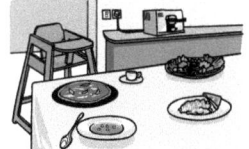

dining room

salle à manger

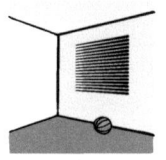

floor

sol

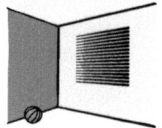

wall

mur

ceiling

plafond

cellar

cave

sauna

sauna

balcony

balcon

terrace

terrasse

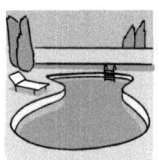

pool

piscine

lawn mower

tondeuse à gazon

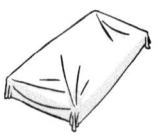

sheet

housse

bedspread

couette

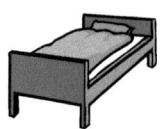

bed

lit

broom

balai

bucket

sceau

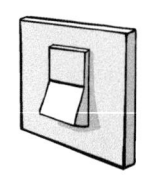

switch

interrupteur

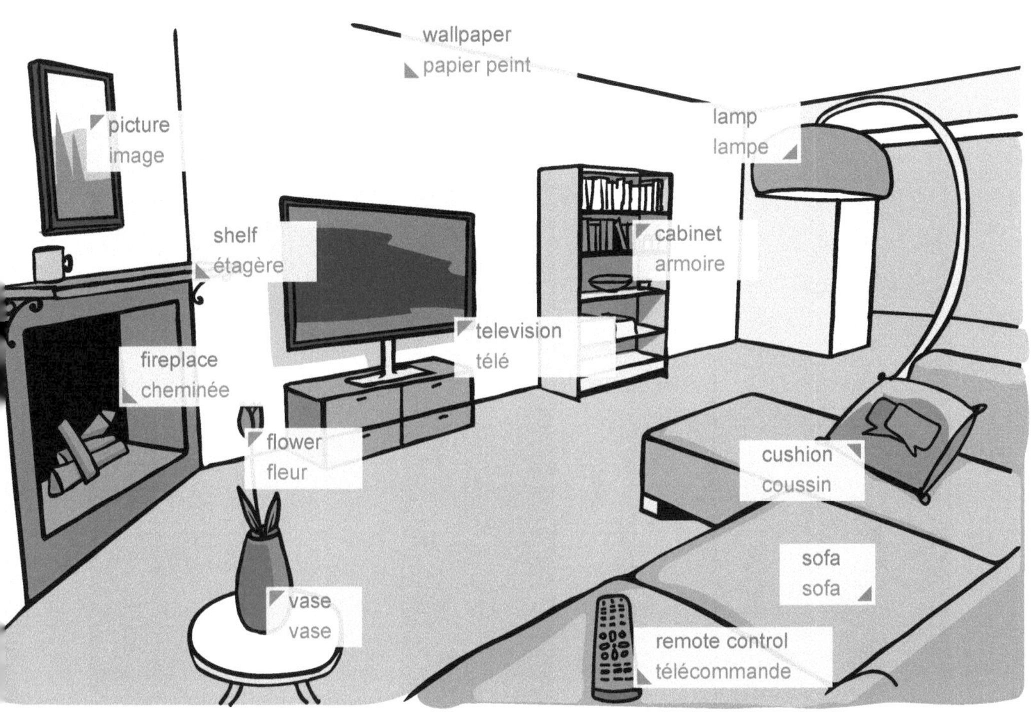

wallpaper
papier peint

picture
image

lamp
lampe

shelf
étagère

cabinet
armoire

fireplace
cheminée

television
télé

flower
fleur

cushion
coussin

vase
vase

sofa
sofa

remote control
télécommande

carpet

tapis

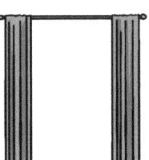

drape

rideau

table

table

chair

chaise

rocking chair

chaise à bascule

armchair

fauteuil

book

livre

blanket

couverture

decoration

décoration

firewood

bois de chauffage

film

film

stereo system

chaîne hi-fi

key

clé

newspaper

journal

painting

peinture

poster

poster

radio

radio

notebook

bloc-notes

vacuum cleaner

aspirateur

cactus

cactus

candle

bougie

kitchen
cuisine

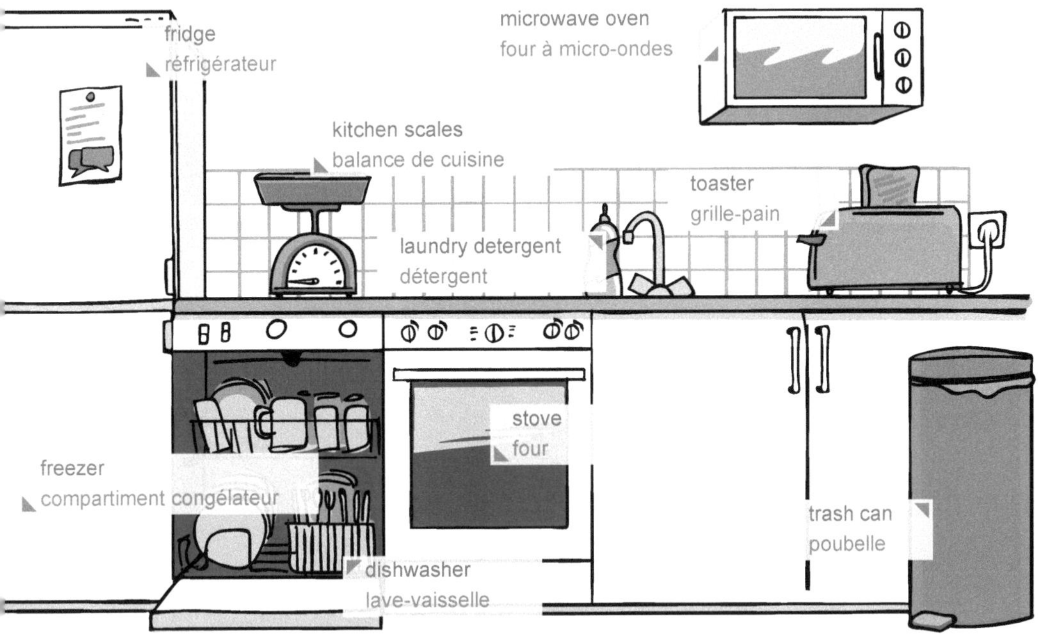
fridge
réfrigérateur
microwave oven
four à micro-ondes
kitchen scales
balance de cuisine
toaster
grille-pain
laundry detergent
détergent
stove
four
freezer
compartiment congélateur
trash can
poubelle
dishwasher
lave-vaisselle

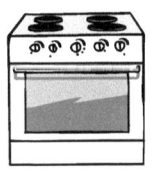

cooker

four

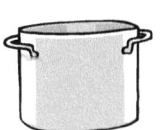

pot

casserole

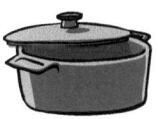

cast-iron pot

marmite

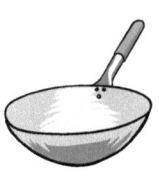

wok / kadai

wok / kadai

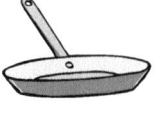

pan

poêle

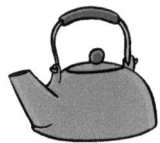

kettle

bouilloire electrique

steamer

cuiseur vapeur

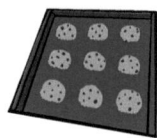

baking tray

plaque de cuisson

crockery

vaisselle

mug

gobelet

bowl

coupe

chopsticks

baguettes

ladle

louche

spatula

spatule

whisk

fouet

strainer

passoire

sieve

tamis

grater

râpe

mortar

mortier

barbecue

barbecue

fireplace

cheminée

chopping board
....
planche à découper

rolling pin
....
rouleau à pâtisserie

corkscrew
....
tire-bouchon

can
....
boîte

can opener
....
ouvre-boîte

oven cloth
....
maniques

sink
....
lavabo

brush
....
brosse

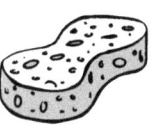

sponge
....
éponge

blender
....
mixeur

deep freezer
....
congélateur

baby bottle
....
biberon

tap
....
robinet

kitchen - cuisine

bathroom

salle de bain

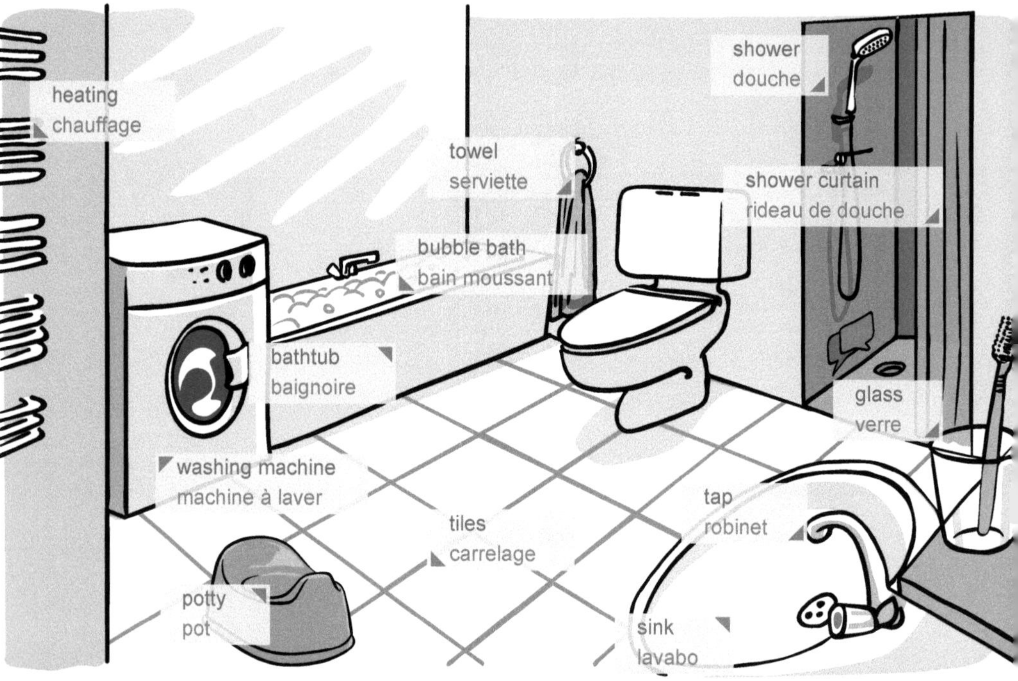
heating
chauffage
towel
serviette
shower
douche
shower curtain
rideau de douche
bubble bath
bain moussant
bathtub
baignoire
washing machine
machine à laver
glass
verre
tap
robinet
tiles
carrelage
potty
pot
sink
lavabo

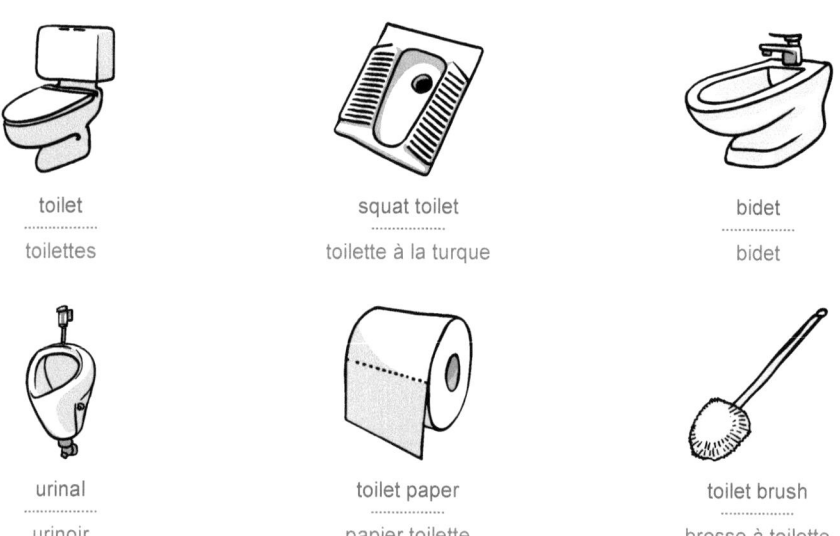

toilet

toilettes

squat toilet

toilette à la turque

bidet

bidet

urinal

urinoir

toilet paper

papier toilette

toilet brush

brosse à toilette

toothbrush

brosse à dents

toothpaste

dentifrice

dental floss

fil dentaire

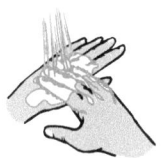

wash

laver

hand shower

douche manuelle

douche

douche intime

basin

vasque

back brush

brosse dorsale

soap

savon

shower gel

gel douche

shampoo

shampooing

flannel

gant de toilette

drain

écoulement

creme

crème

deodorant

déodorant

mirror

miroir

hand mirror

miroir cosmétique

razor

rasoir

shaving foam

mousse à raser

aftershave

après-rasage

comb

peigne

brush

brosse

hair-dryer

sèche-cheveux

hairspray

laque pour cheveux

makeup

fond de teint

lipstick

rouge à lèvres

nail varnish

vernis à ongles

cotton wool

ouate

nail scissors

coupe-ongles

perfume

parfum

washbag

trousse de toilette

stool

tabouret

weighing scales

pèse-personne

bathrobe

peignoir

rubber gloves

gants de nettoyage

tampon

tampon

sanitary towel

serviettes hygiéniques

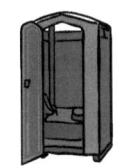

chemical toilet

toilette chimique

kids room
chambre d'enfant

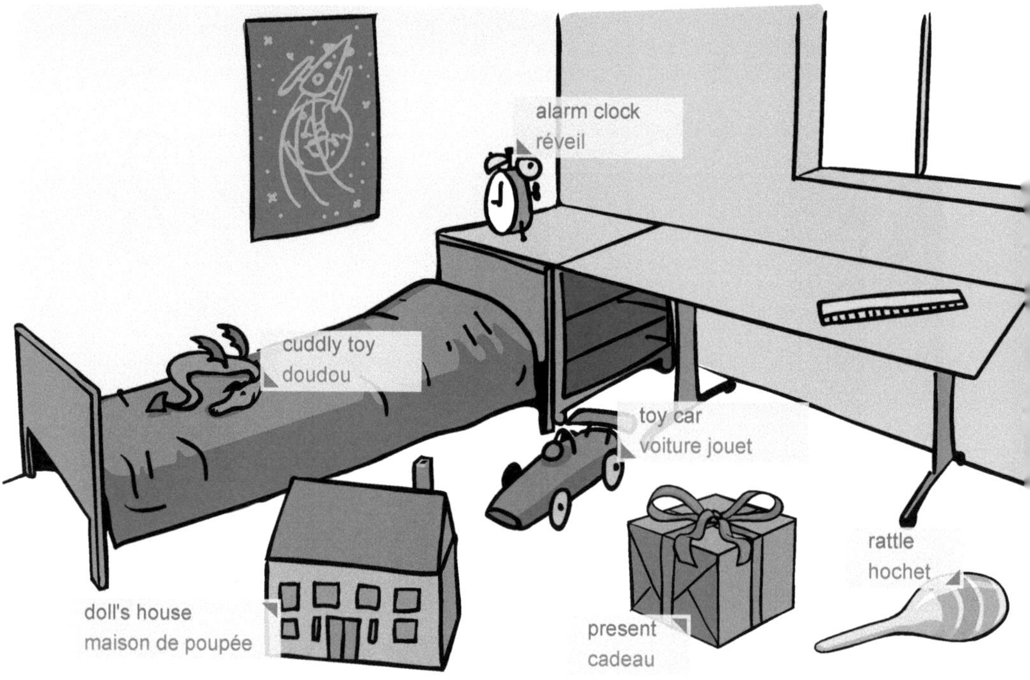
alarm clock
réveil
cuddly toy
doudou
toy car
voiture jouet
rattle
hochet
doll's house
maison de poupée
present
cadeau

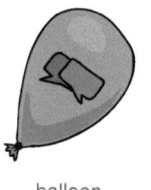

balloon

ballon

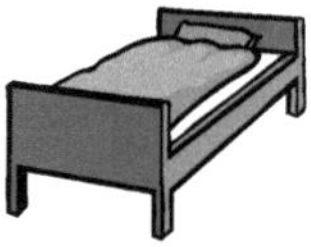

bed

lit

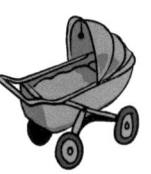

stroller

poussette

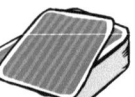

deck of cards

jeu de cartes

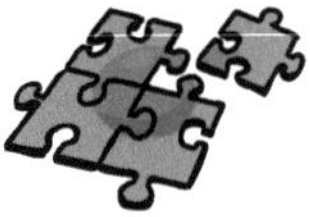

jigsaw

puzzle

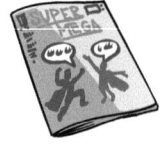

comic

bande dessinée

lego bricks

pièces lego

toy blocks

blocs de construction

action figure

figurine

romper suit

grenouillère

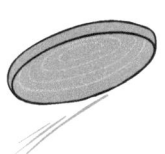

frisbee

frisbee

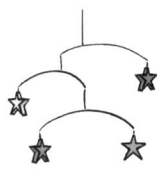

mobile

mobile

board game

jeu de société

dice

dé

model train set

train miniature

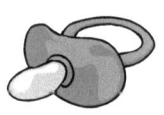

pacifier

sucette

party

fête

picture book

livre d'images

ball

balle

doll

poupée

play

jouer

sandpit

bac à sable

swing

balançoire

toys

jouets

video game console

console de jeu

tricycle

tricycle

teddy bear

ours en peluche

wardrobe

armoire

clothing

vêtements

socks

chaussettes

stockings

bas

tights

collant

scarf
écharpe

umbrella
parapluie

t-shirt
t-shirt

belt
ceinture

boots
bottes

slippers
pantoufles

sneakers
baskets

sandals
sandales

shoes
chaussures

rubber boots
bottes de caoutchouc

underwear
sous-vêtements

bra
soutien-gorge

undershirt
maillot de corps

body

body

pants

pantalon

jeans

jean

skirt

jupe

blouse

chemisier

shirt

chemise

pullover

pull

sweater

sweat à capuche

blazer

veste

jacket

veste

coat

manteau

raincoat

imperméable

costume

costume

dress

robe

wedding dress

robe de mariée

suit
costume

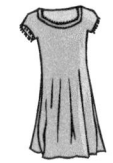

nightgown
chemise de nuit

pajamas
pyjama

sari
sari

headscarf
foulard

turban
turban

burka
burqa

kaftan
caftan

abaya
abaya

swimsuit
maillot de bain

trunks
maillot de bain

shorts
short

tracksuit
tenue d'entraînement

apron
tablier

gloves
gants

button

bouton

glasses

lunettes

bracelet

bracelet

necklace

collier

ring

bague

earring

boucle d'oreille

cap

bonnet

coat hanger

cintre

hat

chapeau

tie

cravate

zip

fermeture éclair

helmet

casque

braces

bretelles

school uniform

uniforme scolaire

uniform

uniforme

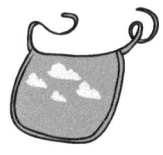

bib

bavoir

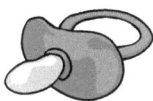

pacifier

sucette

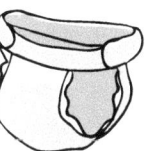

diaper

lange

office

bureau

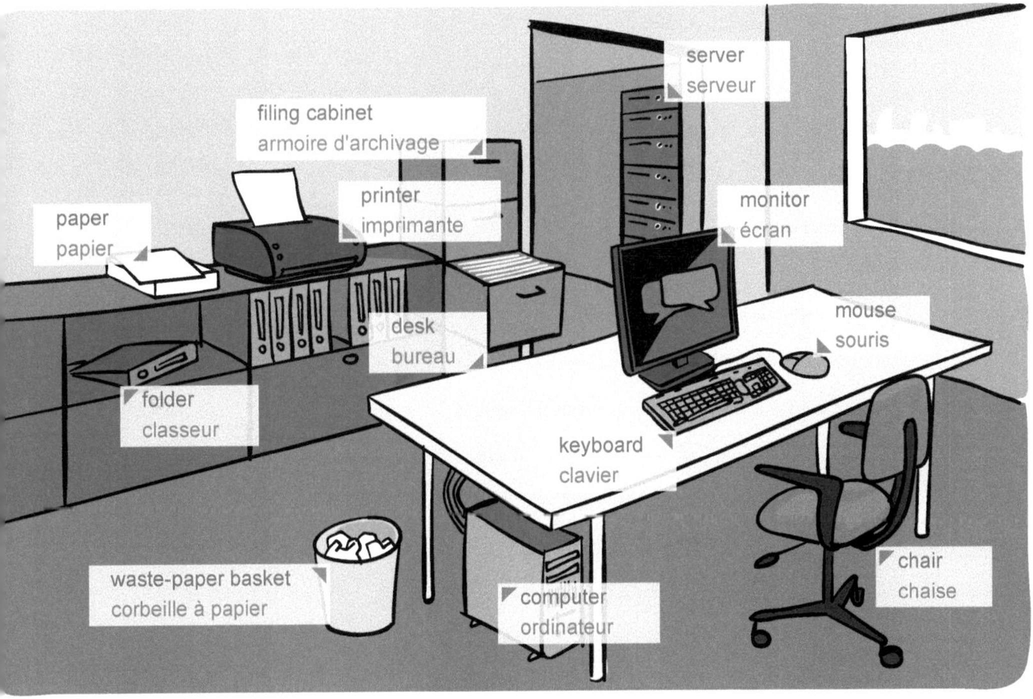

server
serveur
filing cabinet
armoire d'archivage
printer
imprimante
monitor
écran
paper
papier
desk
bureau
mouse
souris
folder
classeur
keyboard
clavier
chair
chaise
waste-paper basket
corbeille à papier
computer
ordinateur

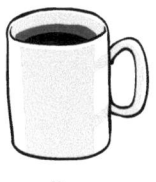

coffee mug

tasse de café

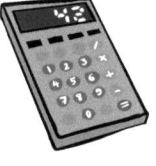

calculator

calculatrice

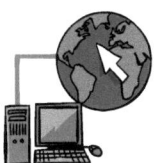

internet

internet

laptop
ordinateur portable

letter
lettre

message
message

cell phone
portable

network
réseau

photocopier
photocopieuse

software
logiciel

telephone
téléphone

plug socket
prise

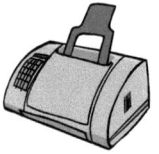

fax machine
fax

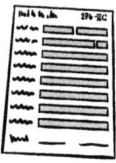

form
formulaire

document
document

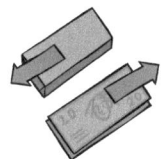

buy

acheter

pay

payer

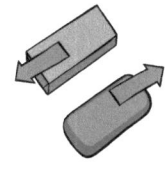

trade

faire du commerce

money

monnaie

 **USD**

dollar

dollar

 **EUR**

euro

euro

 **JPY**

yen

yen

 **RUB**

rouble

rouble

 **CHF**

Swiss franc

franc suisse

 **CNY**

renminbi yuan

renminbi yuan

 **INR**

rupee

roupie

cash point

distributeur automatique

currency exchange office

bureau de change

gold

or

silver

argent

oil

pétrole

energy

énergie

price

prix

contract

contrat

tax

taxe

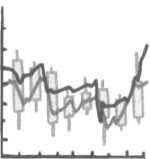

stock

action

work

travailler

employee

employé

employer

employeur

factory

usine

shop

magasin

economy - économie

occupations
professions

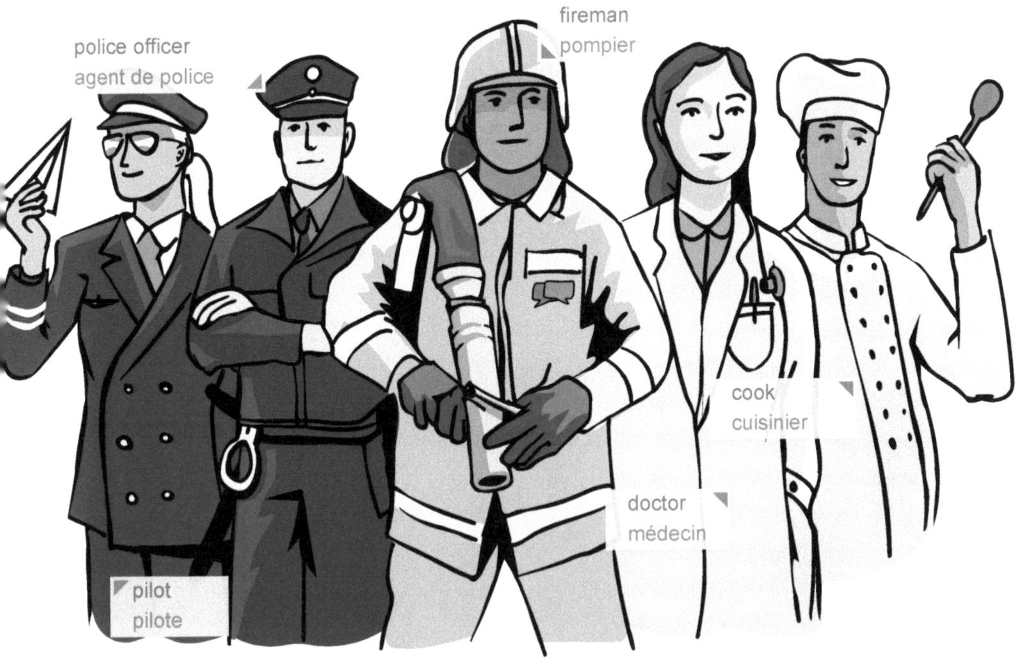
police officer
agent de police
fireman
pompier
cook
cuisinier
doctor
médecin
pilot
pilote

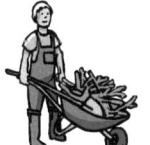

gardener
jardinier

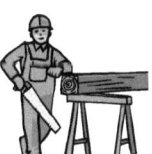

carpenter
menuisier

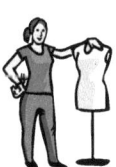

seamstress
couturière

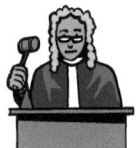

judge
juge

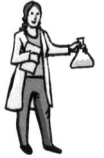

chemist
chimiste

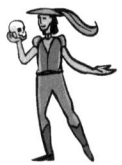

actor
acteur

bus driver

conducteur de bus

taxi driver

chauffeur de taxi

fisherman

pêcheur

cleaning lady

femme de ménage

roofer

couvreur

waiter

serveur

hunter

chasseur

painter

peintre

baker

boulanger

electrician

électricien

builder

ouvrier

engineer

ingénieur

butcher

boucher

plumber

plombier

postman

facteur

soldier

soldat

architect

architecte

cashier

caissier

florist

fleuriste

hairdresser

coiffeur

conductor

contrôleur

mechanic

mécanicien

captain

capitaine

dentist

dentiste

scientist

scientifique

rabbi

rabbin

imam

imam

monk

moine

pastor

prêtre

tools
outils

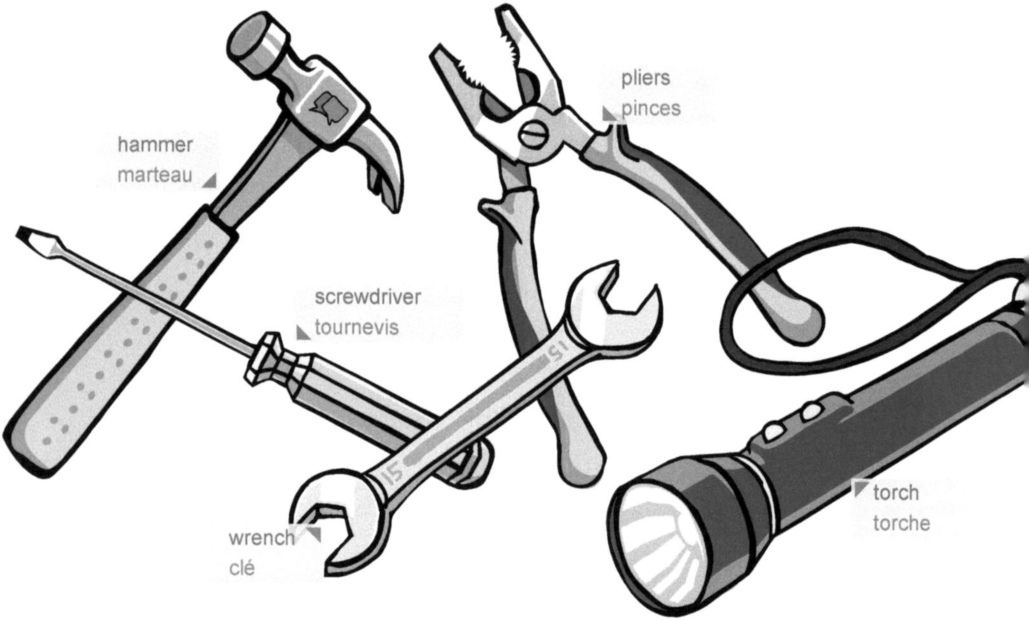
pliers
pinces
hammer
marteau
screwdriver
tournevis
torch
torche
wrench
clé

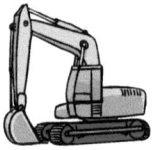

excavator

pelleteuse

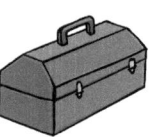

toolbox

boîte à outils

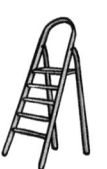

ladder

échelle

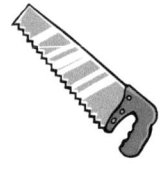

saw

scie

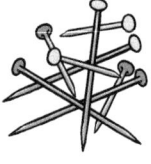

nails

clous

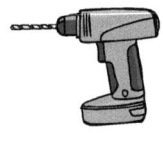

drill

perceuse

repair
réparer

shovel
pelle

Damn!
Mince !

dustpan
pelle

paint can
pot de peinture

screws
vis

musical instruments
instruments de musique

drum set
batterie

loud speaker
haut-parleurs

guitar
guitare

double bass
contrebasse

trumpet
trompette

piano
piano

violin
violon

bass
basse

timpani
timbales

drums
tambour

keyboard
piano électrique

saxophone
saxophone

flute
flûte

microphone
microphone

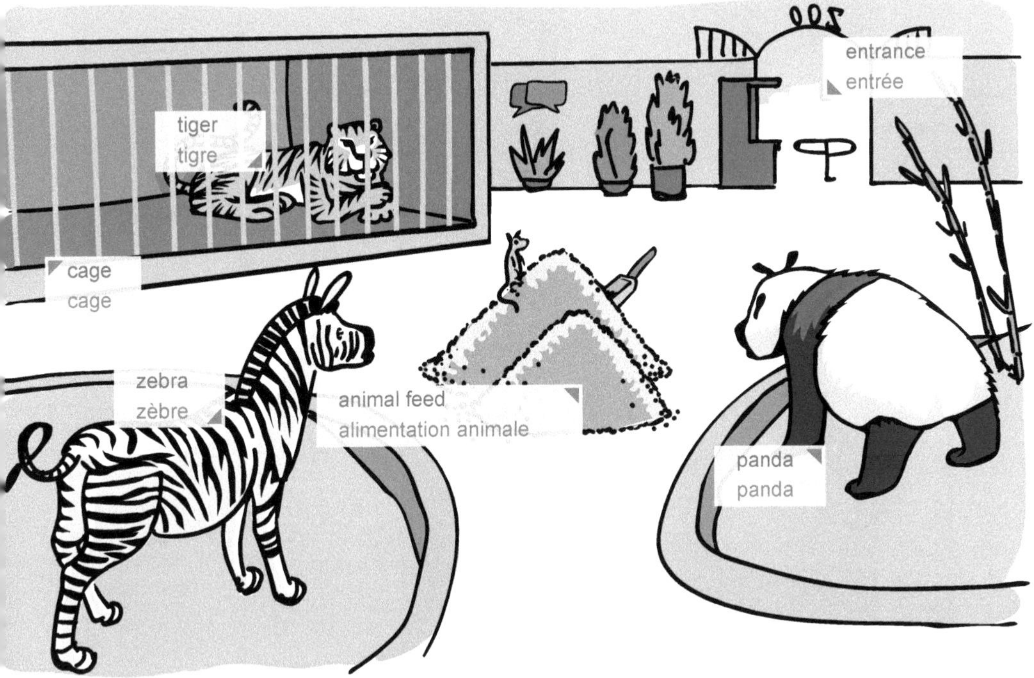

entrance
entrée

tiger
tigre

cage
cage

zebra
zèbre

animal feed
alimentation animale

panda
panda

animals
animaux

elephant
éléphant

kangaroo
kangourou

rhino
rhinocéros

gorilla
gorille

bear
ours

camel

chameau

ostrich

autruche

lion

lion

monkey

singe

flamingo

flamand rose

parrot

perroquet

polar bear

ours polaire

penguin

pingouin

shark

requin

peacock

paon

snake

serpent

crocodile

crocodile

zookeeper

gardien de zoo

seal

phoque

jaguar

jaguar

pony

poney

leopard

léopard

hippo

hippopotame

giraffe

girafe

eagle

aigle

boar

sanglier

fish

poisson

turtle

tortue

walrus

morse

fox

renard

gazelle

gazelle

American football
american Football

cycling
cyclisme

tennis
tennis

basketball
basket-ball

swimming
natation

boxing
boxe

ice hockey
hockey sur glace

soccer
football

badminton
badminton

athletics
athlétisme

handball
handball

skiing
ski

polo
polo

jump
sauter

hug
embrasser

laugh
rire

walk
marcher

sing
chanter

dream
rêver

pray
prier

kiss
faire la bise

write
écrire

draw
dessiner

show
montrer

push
pousser

give
donner

take
prendre

activities - activités

have
avoir

do
faire

be
être

stand
être debout

run
courir

pull
trier

throw
jeter

fall
tomber

lie
être couché

wait
attendre

carry
porter

sit
être assis

get dressed
s'habiller

sleep
dormir

wake up
se réveiller

look at

regarder

cry

pleurer

stroke

caresser

comb

peigner

talk

parler

understand

comprendre

ask

demander

listen

écouter

drink

boire

eat

manger

tidy up

ranger

love

aimer

cook

cuire

drive

conduire

fly

voler

activities - activités

sail

faire de la voile

calculate

calculer

read

lire

learn

apprendre

work

travailler

marry

se marier

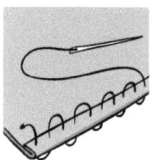

sew

coudre

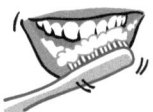

brush teeth

brosser les dents

kill

tuer

smoke

fumer

send

envoyer

activities - activités

grandmother
grand-mère

grandfather
grand-père

father
père

mother
mère

baby
bébé

daughter
fille

son
fils

guest

hôte

aunt

tante

uncle

oncle

brother

frère

sister

sœur

family - famille

67

body
corps

forehead
front
eye
œil
face
visage
chin
menton
finger
doigt
hand
main
breast
poitrine
arm
bras
shoulder
épaule
leg
jambe

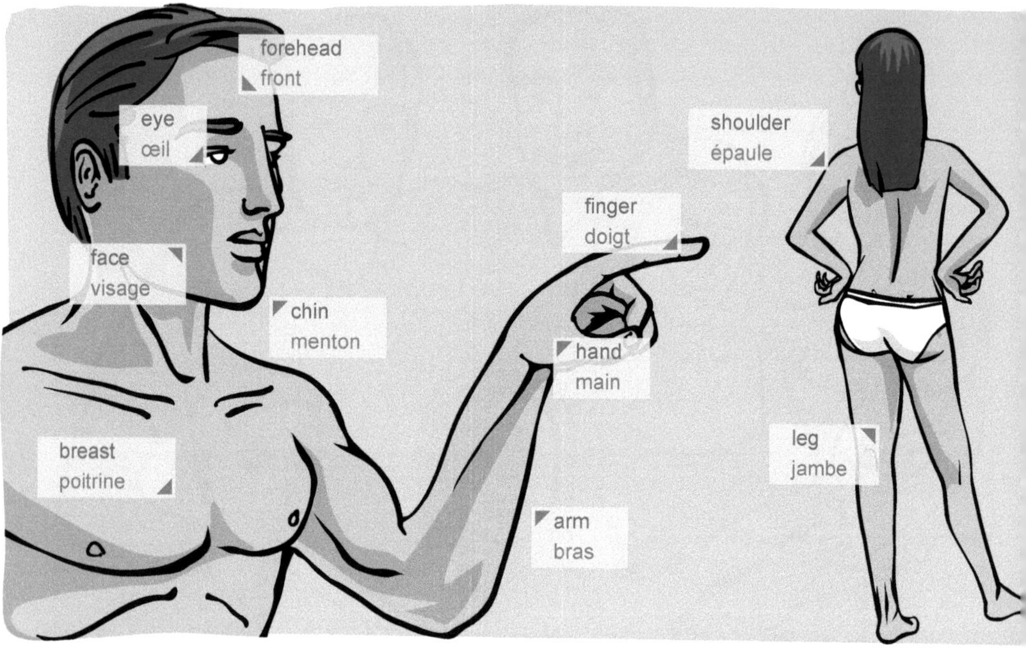

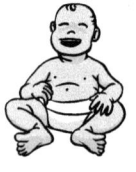

baby

bébé

man

homme

woman

femme

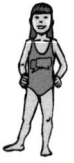

girl

fille

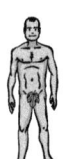

boy

garçon

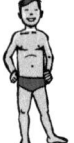

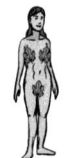

head

tête

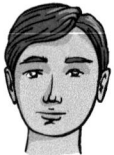

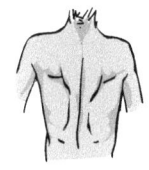

back

dos

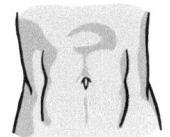

belly

ventre

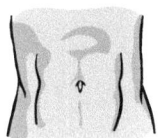

navel

nombril

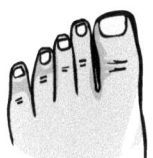

toe

orteil

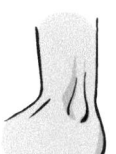

heel

talon

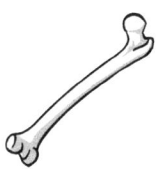

bone

os

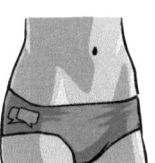

hip

hanche

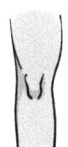

knee

genou

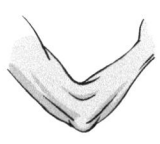

elbow

coude

nose

nez

buttocks

fesses

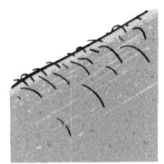

skin

peau

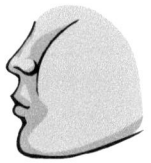

cheek

joue

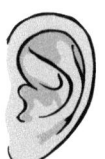

ear

oreille

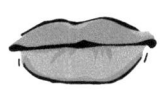

lip

lèvre

mouth

bouche

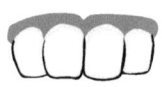

tooth

dent

tongue

langue

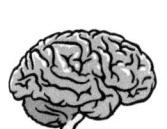

brain

cerveau

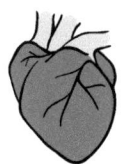

heart

cœur

muscle

muscle

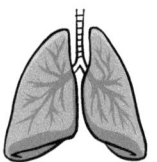

lung

poumons

liver

foie

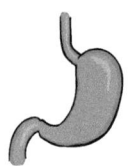

stomach

estomac

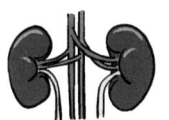

kidneys

reins

sex

rapport sexuel

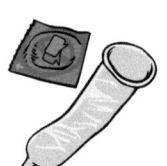

condom

préservatif

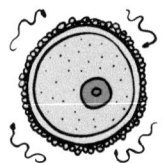

ovum

ovule

semen

sperme

pregnancy

grossesse

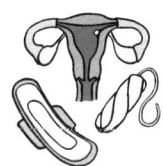

menstruation
menstruation

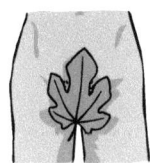

vagina
vagin

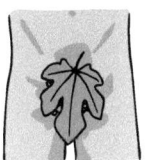

penis
pénis

eyebrow
sourcil

hair
cheveux

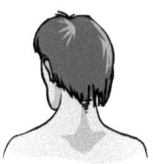

neck
cou

hospital
hôpital

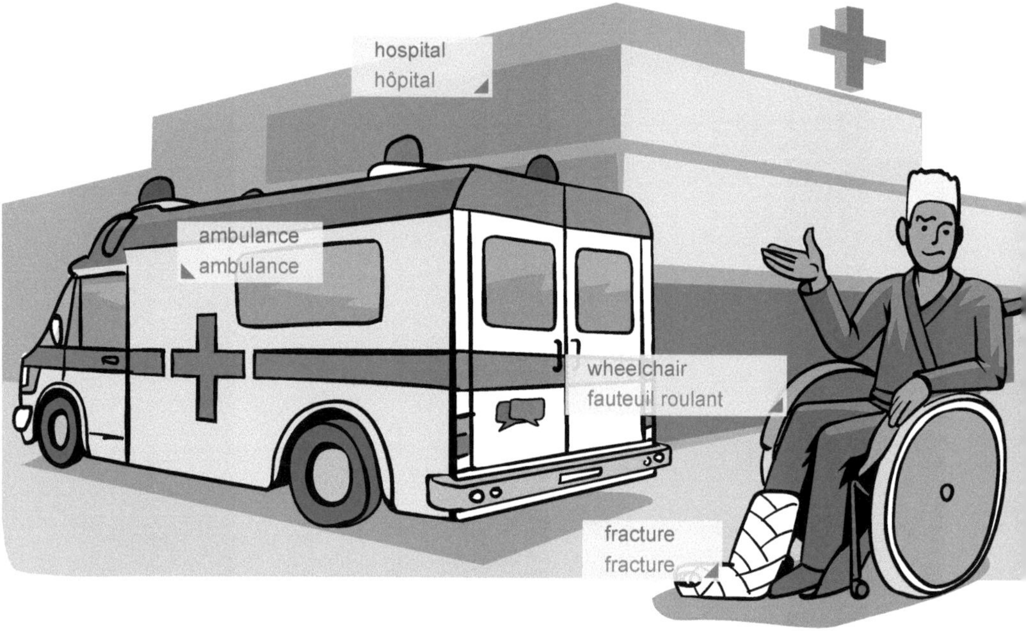

hospital
hôpital
ambulance
ambulance
wheelchair
fauteuil roulant
fracture
fracture

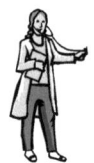

doctor
médecin

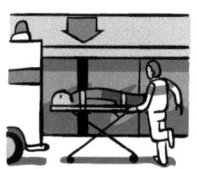

emergency room
service des urgences

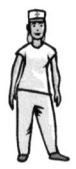

nurse
infirmière

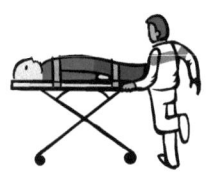

emergency
urgence

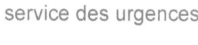

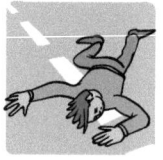

unconscious
inconscient

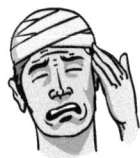

pain
douleur

injury

blessure

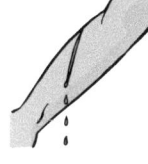

bleeding

hémorragie

heart attack

crise cardiaque

stroke

attaque cérébrale

allergy

allergie

cough

toux

fever

fièvre

flu

grippe

diarrhea

diarrhée

headache

mal de tête

cancer

cancer

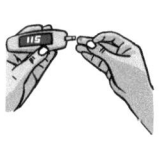

diabetes

diabète

surgeon

chirurgien

scalpel

scalpel

operation

opération

CT
CT

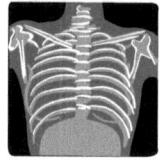

x-ray
radiographie

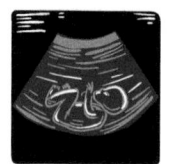

ultrasound
échographie

face mask
masque

disease
maladie

waiting room
salle d'attente

crutch
béquille

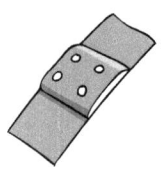

plaster
pansement

bandage
pansement

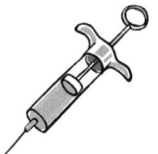

injection
injection

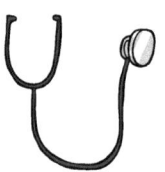

stethoscope
stéthoscope

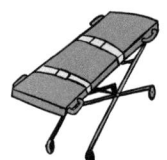

stretcher
brancard

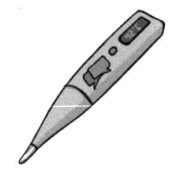

clinical thermometer
thermomètre

birth
accouchement

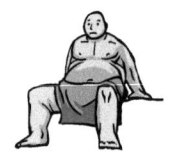

overweight
surcharge pondérale

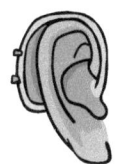

hearing aid

appareil auditif

disinfectant

désinfectant

infection

infection

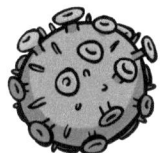

virus

virus

HIV / AIDS

VIH / sida

medicine

médicament

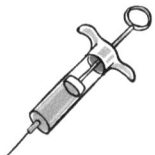

vaccination

vaccination

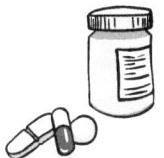

tablets

comprimés

pill

pilule

emergency call

appel d'urgence

blood pressure monitor

tensiomètre

ill / healthy

malade / sain

Help!

Au secours !

alarm

alarme

assault

assaut

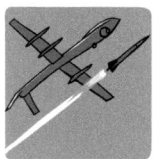

attack

attaque

danger

danger

emergency exit

sortie de secours

Fire!

Au feu!

fire extinguisher

extincteur

accident

accident

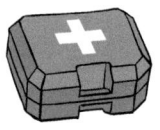

first-aid kit

trousse de premier secours

SOS

SOS

police

police

Europe

Europe

North America

Amérique du Nord

South America

Amérique du Sud

Africa

Afrique

Asia

Asie

Australia

Australie

Atlantic

Océan atlantique

Pacific

Océan pacifique

Indian Ocean

Océan indien

Antarctic Ocean

Océan antarctique

Arctic Ocean

Océan arctique

North pole

pôle nord

South pole
pôle sud

Antarctica
Antarctique

earth
terre

land
pays

sea
mer

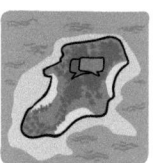

island
île

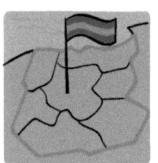

nation
nation

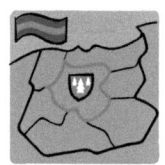

state
état

clock face

cadran

hour hand

aiguille des heures

minute hand

aiguille des minutes

second hand

aiguille des secondes

What time is it?

Quelle heure est-il ?

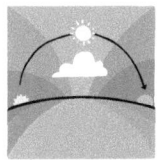

day

jour

time

temps

now

maintenant

digital watch

montre digitale

minute

minute

hour

heure

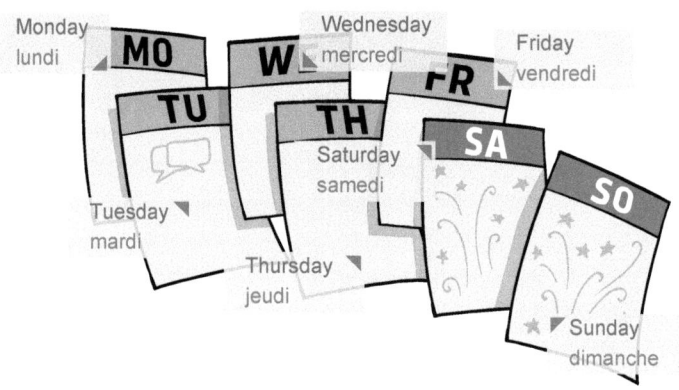

Monday
lundi
Wednesday
mercredi
Friday
vendredi
Tuesday
mardi
Saturday
samedi
Thursday
jeudi
Sunday
dimanche

yesterday

hier

today

aujourd'hui

tomorrow

demain

morning

matin

noon

midi

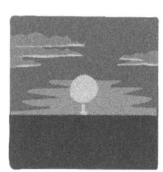

evening

soir

workdays

jours ouvrables

weekend

week-end

rain
pluie

rainbow
arc-en-ciel

wind
vent

snow
neige

spring
printemps

summer
été

fall
automne

winter
hiver

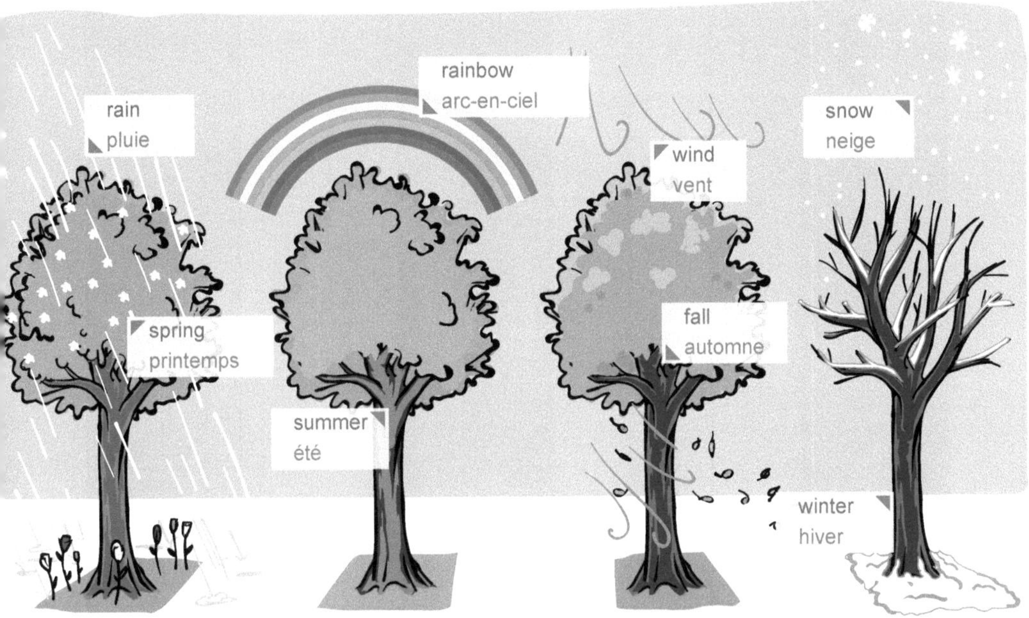

weather forecast

météo

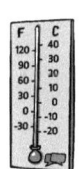

thermometer

thermomètre

sunshine

lumière du soleil

cloud

nuage

fog

brouillard

humidity

humidité

lightning

foudre

thunder

tonnerre

storm

tempête

hail

grêle

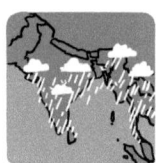

monsoon

mousson

flood

inondation

ice

glace

January

janvier

February

février

March

mars

April

avril

May

mai

June

juin

July

juillet

August

août

year - année

September
....
septembre

October
....
octobre

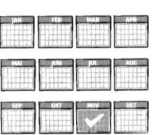

November
....
novembre

December
....
décembre

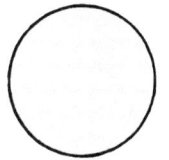

circle
....
cercle

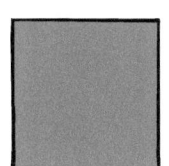

square
....
carré

rectangle
....
rectangle

triangle
....
triangle

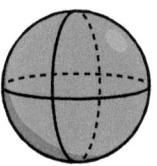

sphere
....
sphère

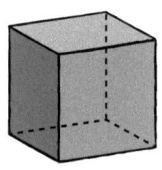

cube
....
cube

white

blanc

yellow

jaune

orange

orange

pink

rose

red

rouge

purple

violet

blue

bleu

green

vert

brown

marron

gray

gris

black

noir

a lot / a little

beaucoup / peu

angry / calm

fâché / calme

beautiful / ugly

joli / laid

beginning / end

début / fin

big / small

grand / petit

bright / dark

clair / obscure

brother / sister

frère / soeur

clean / dirty

propre / sale

complete / incomplete

complet / incomplet

day / night

jour / nuit

dead / alive

mort / vivant

wide / narrow

large / étroit

edible / inedible

comestible / incomestible

evil / kind

méchant / gentil

excited / bored

excité / ennuyé

fat / thin

gros / mince

first / last

premier / dernier

friend / enemy

ami / ennemi

full / empty

plein / vide

hard / soft

dur / souple

heavy / light

lourd / léger

hunger / thirst

faim / soif

ill / healthy

malade / sain

illegal / legal

illégal / légal

intelligent / stupid

intelligent / stupide

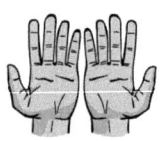

left / right

gauche / droite

near / far

proche / loin

new / used

nouveau / usé

nothing / something

rien / quelque chose

old / young

vieux / jeune

on / off

marche / arrêt

open / closed

ouvert / fermé

quiet / loud

faible / fort

rich / poor

riche / pauvre

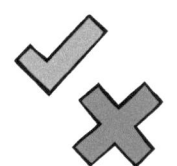

right / wrong

correct / incorrect

rough / smooth

rugueux / lisse

sad / happy

triste / heureux

short / long

court / long

slow / fast

lent / rapide

wet / dry

mouillé / sec

warm / cool

chaud / froid

war / peace

guerre / paix

opposites - oppositions

0

zero

zéro

1

one

un / une

2

two

deux

3

three

trois

4

four

quatre

5

five

cinq

6

six

six

7

seven

sept

8

eight

huit

9

nine

neuf

10

ten

dix

11

eleven

onze

12

twelve

douze

13

thirteen

treize

14

fourteen

quatorze

15

fifteen

quinze

16

sixteen

seize

17

seventeen

dix-sept

18

eighteen

dix-huit

19

nineteen

dix-neuf

20

twenty

vingt

100

hundred

cent

1.000

thousand

mille

1.000.000

million

million

English
....
anglais

American English
....
anglais américain

Chinese Mandarin
....
chinois mandarin

Hindi
....
hindi

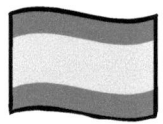

Spanish
....
espagnol

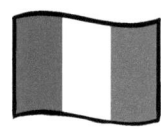

French
....
français

Arabic
....
arabe

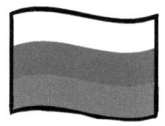

Russian
....
russe

Portuguese
....
portugais

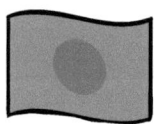

Bengali
....
bengali

German
....
allemand

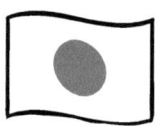

Japanese
....
japonais

I
je

you
tu

he / she / it
il / elle / ce, c', cela

we
nous

you
vous

they
ils / elles

who?
Qui ?

what?
Quoi ?

how?
Comment ?

where?
Où ?

when?
Quand ?

name
nom

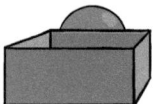

behind

derrière

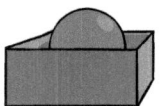

in

dans

in front of

devant

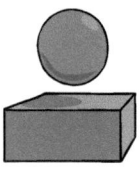

over

au-dessus

on

sur

under

en-dessous

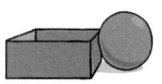

beside

à côté de

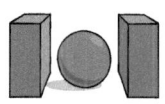

between

entre

place

lieu